JULY

Ellen Jackson

Illustrated by
Pat DeWitt and Robin DeWitt

Charlesbridge

To Ray King and Kale Starbird
—E. J.
To two very influential people,
our teachers Ed Saffel and Ted Brower
—P. D. & R. D.

Did You Know?

July is a month of brilliant color. The fields and woodlands are lush and green. Scarlet tanagers and goldfinches dart among the treetops. Black-eyed Susans blaze orange-yellow in the meadows or in empty lots, and bright blue dragonflies flit above ponds and streams.

The gillyflower, which has sweet-smelling blossoms in a variety of colors, is also called the July flower because it appears during this month. In his play *The Winter's Tale*, William Shakespeare called gillyflowers "the fairest flowers" of the season.

Fluffy white clouds drift across the sky like sailboats on the ocean. In some places, July brings thunderstorms and showers. An English proverb says, "If the first of July be rainy weather, / It will rain, more or less, for four weeks together."

In the woods, food is plentiful. Bullfrogs squat near streams, catching flies. Chipmunks nibble snippets of grass, and bears roam in search of wild blackberries.

In most countries in the Northern Hemisphere, July is the hottest month of the year. The highest temperature ever recorded in the United States—134 degrees Fahrenheit—occurred in Death Valley, California, on July 10, 1913.

July is the first full month of summer. People often plan picnics or go hiking in the mountains in July, which is one of the best months to enjoy the outdoors. It is the month for watching fireworks, building campfires, and roasting marshmallows on sticks. It is also a time for going barefoot, dashing through twirling sprinklers, and looking for fireflies after dark.

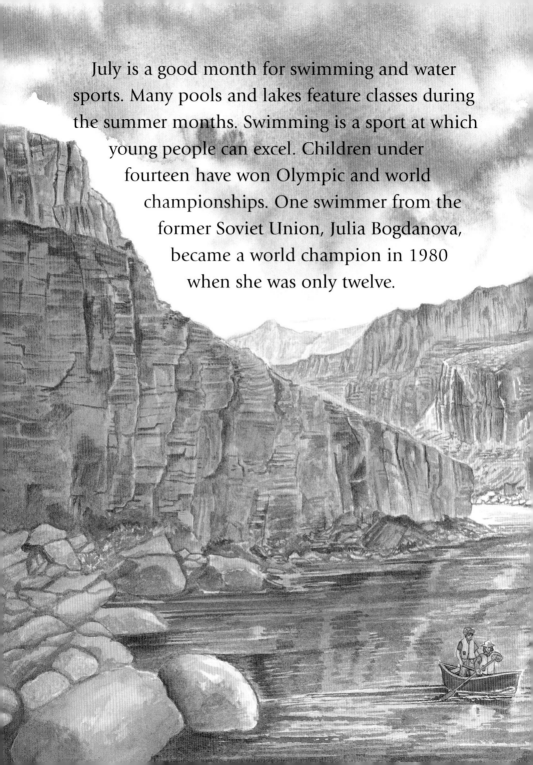

July is a good month for swimming and water sports. Many pools and lakes feature classes during the summer months. Swimming is a sport at which young people can excel. Children under fourteen have won Olympic and world championships. One swimmer from the former Soviet Union, Julia Bogdanova, became a world champion in 1980 when she was only twelve.

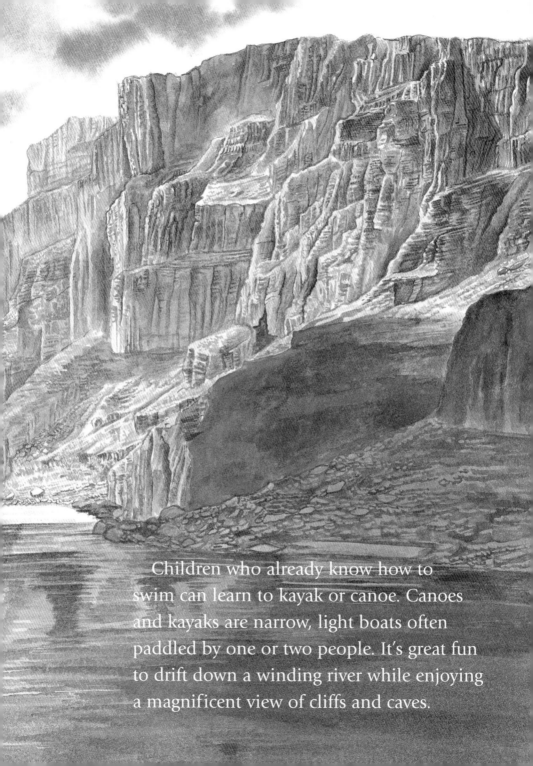

Children who already know how to swim can learn to kayak or canoe. Canoes and kayaks are narrow, light boats often paddled by one or two people. It's great fun to drift down a winding river while enjoying a magnificent view of cliffs and caves.

The July Birthstone

The birthstone for July is the ruby, the rarest of all gems. In ancient Eastern legends, rubies were said to contain a life-giving drop of blood from Mother Earth. The Romans believed that rubies belonged to Mars, the god of war. They thought that the bold red color of this stone represented power and authority.

The July Flower

If you were born in July, your special flower is the water lily. People have admired water lilies for thousands of years. The ancient Egyptians placed these flowers on their altars and gave them to important visitors as a sign of friendship and goodwill. The ancient Greeks dedicated water lilies to the nymphs, or nature spirits, who were said to live in rivers, lakes, or ponds.

The July Zodiac

Cancer, the crab, is the astrological sign for people with birthdays from June 22 to July 22. People born under Cancer are said to be warm and caring, although sometimes they can be too emotional. They love to be around family and friends and are team players. A Cancer loves food and always has a good appetite.

The sign for people born from July 23 to August 22 is Leo, the lion. Those born under Leo want to be treated like royalty. They are natural leaders and fast learners. It is said that a Leo can get anyone to do almost anything, although he or she can sometimes be too bossy.

The Calendar

July is the seventh month of the year and has thirty-one days. In ancient Rome, the year began in March, not January. July was then the fifth month and was called *Quintilis*, which means "fifth" in Latin.

In 44 B.C., the month's name was changed to *Julius* in honor of Julius Caesar, a great soldier, general, and ruler of Rome. *Quintilis* was renamed because it was the month in which Julius Caesar was born in 100 B.C.

Until the seventeenth century, the month had a number of different spellings, including Julio, Iulie, and Iule. By 1689, it had acquired its current spelling—July.

Sun, Sky, and Weather

July days are sweet with clover and can be as lazy as a dog drowsing in the sun. Big, cottony clouds make patches of shade on the ground as they drift overhead.

When darker clouds appear, they sometimes bring storms that drench the earth. Lightning flashes, and thunder roars, trailing off into a low, distant rumble.

By July, the sun is edging south in the sky. In the northern United States, there are forty fewer minutes of daylight at the end of July than there are at the end of June.

The prairie is hot and dry. When the air is calm, clumps of bushes seem to shimmer in the distance. The shimmering is an optical illusion, called a mirage, that is caused by the intense heat.

In the desert, hot winds blow. The temperature often reaches one hundred degrees before noon.

The July moon has been called the hay moon by some Native American people because it comes at the time of the hay harvest. The Anglo-Saxons, who settled in Britain in the fifth and sixth centuries, had several names for July, including *Maedd monath*, or meadow month, and *Lida Aefter*, or second mild month.

Animals in July

July's warm weather is good for most living things, but it is especially good for insects. Bees dart from flower to flower, collecting nectar to make honey. Ants dig tunnels and gather food. Dragonflies flit through the air, catching smaller insects as they fly.

In July, male crickets chirp to attract females and warn other males away. They make their sounds by scraping one wing against the other. The chirping of the snowy tree cricket, an insect found throughout North America, speeds up on warm nights. If you hear one, count the number of chirps in a fifteen-second period. Add forty, and you will get the current temperature in degrees Fahrenheit.

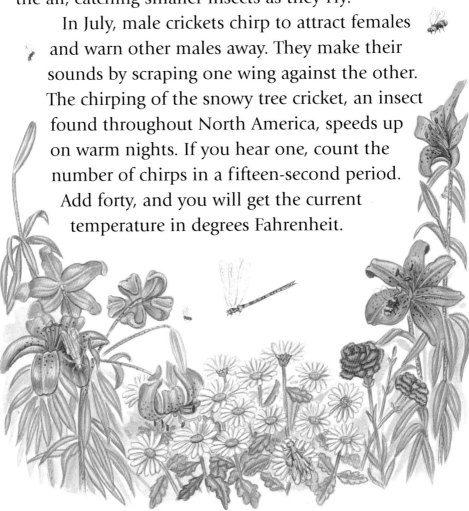

In southern California, Costa's hummingbird can be found sipping from a bird feeder. Hummingbirds weigh only about as much as a penny, and they can fly backward, sideways, or upside-down.

In the desert, cottontail rabbits spend most July afternoons in the shade. They come out in the morning and evening to look for food. Sometimes small groups of Harris's hawks gather together to hunt them. If a rabbit tries to hide in a bush, one hawk will scare it out while the others wait to attack.

In the mountains, male deer, called bucks, have new crowns of antlers to replace the ones that fell off during the previous winter. Bears visit mountain garbage dumps to look for food. If several bears are together, the biggest one always feeds first. Bears also eat beetles, ants, fish, berries, bark, grass, mice, frogs, honey, and even an occasional stick or pebble. They are especially fond of mayflies and will scoop them up by the hundreds.

In Wyoming, yellow-brown prairie dogs sit beside their burrows, enjoying the summer weather. Meriwether Lewis and William Clark, nineteenth-century explorers, called these rodents "barking squirrels." Prairie dogs yip like puppies, touching noses and patting one another whenever they meet. They wag their stubby tails up and down instead of from side to side. Prairie-dog towns once spread for hundreds of miles on the prairies. The towns were considered a nuisance by ranchers, and now only a few small colonies are left.

Plants in July

Wildflowers are everywhere in July. Blue chicory and
Queen Anne's lace appear along the roadways.
Jewelweed and sweetbrier bloom in fields and thickets.
Tall sunflowers bloom in the Midwest in July.
These flowers may grow ten feet high or more.
Their heads follow the sun as it crosses the
sky each day. When summer is over, the centers
of the flowers turn black and seeds appear.

July is a time for walks in the woods. If you go walking, look for an old tree stump with a smooth surface and count the dark rings to find the age of the tree. Each year, the trunk of a tree grows thicker and produces both a light ring and a dark ring.

Rings are thick in years when the tree has received the right amount of sunlight and rain. They are thin in years when rain has been scarce or other growing conditions unfavorable. Scars in the wood may show when the tree was damaged by a forest fire or insects.

Cool places are hard to find in the desert during July. Mesquite trees are one source of shade for mice and rabbits. Native Americans used to gather mesquite beans for food and used the wood of the plant for cooking and making tool handles.

In the city, daisies grow in vacant lots and even in cracks in the concrete. Their name comes from the phrase *day's eye*. In folklore, the yellow center of the daisy was thought to represent the summer sun.

Special Days

Independence-Day Celebrations

Many countries around the world have special days to mark the beginning of their existence as free, independent states. Sometimes these days recognize an important battle or an act of rebellion against a ruling power. Sometimes they mark the beginning of a period of national identity. Countries that celebrate their independence in July include France, Canada, Venezuela, Argentina, Belgium, Colombia, Peru, Egypt, Ghana, and the United States.

Independence-day festivities include parties, speeches, and fireworks. Military bands play patriotic songs, and children march in their school uniforms. Folk dancers perform, and men on prancing horses do acrobatic tricks. People enjoy special food, and in some countries, picnics or outdoor barbecues are part of the fun.

Independence Day in America

Each year on July 4, Americans celebrate the birth of their nation. For many years before 1776, American colonists were unhappy under British rule. Many of them felt the tax laws passed by the English were unfair because the colonists had no representatives in England's Parliament to express their point of view.

A group of patriots, including George Washington, Patrick Henry, Thomas Jefferson, and Benjamin Franklin, began to write and speak about the need for independence. Soon there was widespread support for this idea, and Thomas Jefferson was chosen to write the Declaration of Independence. Others made a few changes, and the declaration was adopted in Philadelphia on July 4, 1776.

The Declaration of Independence states that governments should rule according to the will of their citizens. This idea is the basis for democracy in the United States, and it has inspired people around the world to strive for freedom.

Many important events have occurred on July 4 in other years. On July 4, 1826, John Adams and Thomas Jefferson, signers of the Declaration of Independence and the second and third presidents of the United States, died within hours of one another. On July 4, 1884, the Statue of Liberty was formally presented to the United States minister to France, Levi Parsons Morton, on behalf of the people of France. The statue, which stands on Liberty Island in New York Harbor, has become a symbol of freedom for people everywhere.

Today, the Fourth of July holiday is observed all over the United States. Many families have picnics and barbecues, and towns and cities celebrate this day with parades, concerts, and fireworks.

Famous July Events

On July 14, 1789, in Paris, France, an angry mob stormed and captured the royal prison, which was called the Bastille. For years, the kings of France had imprisoned whomever they chose. By capturing the Bastille and later tearing down its walls, the people expressed their hatred of tyranny. Today Bastille Day is a national holiday in France, celebrated with parades, speeches, and fireworks.

From July 1 to July 3, 1863, a major battle of the American Civil War was fought near the town of Gettysburg, Pennsylvania. More than fifty thousand Union and Confederate soldiers were killed or wounded in the fighting. Later Abraham Lincoln delivered his famous Gettysburg Address at the site of the battle.

On July 2, 1964, President Lyndon Johnson signed the Civil Rights Act. The act prohibited racial, religious, or sex discrimination in the use of public facilities (such as drinking fountains, bathrooms, and pools), in employment, and in the registration of voters. It also gave the federal government the power to enforce laws against such discrimination.

On July 16, 1969, Apollo 11, a manned spacecraft, blasted off for the moon. On board were Neil Armstrong, Edwin "Buzz" Aldrin, and Michael Collins. On July 20, 1969, Neil Armstrong became the first person to walk on the moon. After gathering moon rocks and soil and taking photographs, the three astronauts returned safely to the earth.

Birthdays

Many famous people were born in July.

July 1, 1961

Member of the royal
family of Great Britain and
popular humanitarian.

July 2, 1908

First African American
to serve on the United
States Supreme Court.

July 5, 1810

Better known as P. T.
Barnum. American
showman and owner of a
circus advertised as "The
Greatest Show on Earth."

July 12, 1817

American author and
philosopher. His most
famous book is *Walden*.

Rembrandt van Rijn

July 15, 1606

Famous Dutch artist.
His painting *The Night
Watch* is one of the
best-known paintings
in the world.

Ida Bell Wells-Barnett

July 16, 1862

U.S. journalist, civil-
rights activist, and
antilynching crusader.

Nelson Mandela

July 18, 1918

Civil-rights activist
and president of
South Africa.

John Glenn

July 21, 1921

First American astronaut
to orbit the earth. He
later became a United
States senator.

Amelia Earhart

July 24, 1897

First woman to cross
the Atlantic ocean
flying an airplane solo.

Emily Brontë

July 30, 1818

Novelist and author
of *Wuthering Heights*.

A July Story

When Julius Caesar was in his twenties, he was captured by pirates who roamed the Mediterranean Sea. But Caesar was not afraid of the pirates. At night, he commanded his captors to keep quiet so that he could sleep.

The pirates demanded twenty talents of gold for Caesar's ransom. They threatened to kill him if he could not pay.

Caesar replied proudly, "What! Only twenty talents? I will give you fifty talents for my life!"

While messengers were sent for the money, Caesar joked with his guards. He told them he would come back and take them all prisoner and get the money back as well.

The pirates laughed at the young man's threat. But a few weeks after his release, Caesar hired some ships, pursued the pirates, and captured the entire band.

Later Caesar became a great general who conquered Italy, France, and Spain, and won victories in Greece, Egypt, and Africa. He was also a great writer and historian.

AUTHOR'S NOTE

This book gives an overview of the month of July. But nature does not follow a strict schedule. The mating and migration of animals, the blooming of plants, and other natural events vary from year to year, or occur earlier or later in different places.

The zodiac sections of this book are included just for fun as part of the folklore of the month and should not be taken as accurate descriptions of any real people.

The July story was adapted from *Plutarch: Ten Famous Lives*, translated by John Dryden and edited by Charles Alexander Robinson, Jr. (New York: E.P. Dutton & Co., 1962.)

Published by Charlesbridge Publishing
85 Main Street, Watertown, MA 02472
(617) 926-0329
www.charlesbridge.com

Illustrations done in watercolor on Arches
  hot-press paper
Display type and text type set in Giovanni
Color separations made by Sung In Printing,
  South Korea
Printed and bound by Sung In Printing,
  South Korea
Production supervision by Brian G. Walker
Designed by Diane M. Earley

**Library of Congress
Cataloging-in-Publication Data**

Jackson, Ellen B., 1943-
  July/Ellen Jackson; illustrated by
  Pat DeWitt and Robin DeWitt.
    p.cm.—(It happens in the month of)
  ISBN 0-88106-920-5 (hardcover)
  1. July—Folklore. 2. July—Juvenile
  literature. I. DeWitt, Pat, ill. II. DeWitt,
  Robin, ill. III. Title.

  GR930.J335   2002
  398'.33—dc21   2001023507

Printed in South Korea
10 9 8 7 6 5 4 3 2 1